PIONEERS IN HEALTH AND MEDICINE

The Life of
Elizabeth Blackwell

PIONEERS  IN HEALTH AND MEDICINE

The Life of
Elizabeth Blackwell

Elizabeth Schleichert
Illustrated by Antonio Castro

Twenty-First Century Books

A Division of Henry Holt and Co., Inc.

Frederick, Maryland

Published by
Twenty-First Century Books
A Division of Henry Holt and Co., Inc.
38 South Market Street
Frederick, Maryland 21701

Text Copyright © 1992
Elizabeth Schleichert

Illustrations Copyright © 1992
Twenty-First Century Books
A Division of Henry Holt and Co., Inc.

Printed in Mexico

10 9 8 7 6 5 4 3 2 1

Library of Congress Cataloging in Publication Data
Schleichert, Elizabeth
The Life of Elizabeth Blackwell
Illustrated by Antonio Castro
(A Pioneers in Health and Medicine Book)
Includes index and bibliographical references.
Summary: Examines the life of the first female doctor
in the United States, who worked to open the field of
medicine to women.
1. Blackwell, Elizabeth, 1821-1910—Juvenile literature.
2. Physicians—New York (State)—Biography—Juvenile
literature. 3. Women physicians—New York (State)—
Biography—Juvenile literature. [1. Blackwell, Elizabeth,
1821-1910. 2. Women physicians. 3. Physicians.]
I. Castro, Antonio, 1941— ill. II. Title. III. Series: Pioneers in
Health and Medicine.
R154.B623S35 1991 610'.92—dc20 [B] 91-29853 CIP AC
ISBN 0-941477-66-5

Contents

1

A Woman's Career

On May 12, 1857, a small crowd collected on the sun-flecked cobblestones before the old Dutch house at 64 Bleecker Street in New York City. The elegant row house had been fitted up as a hospital. The guests invited to its opening had been waiting patiently to examine its transformation from a private home to a house of healing.

Finally, the hospital doors were opened. As they shouldered through the graceful entrance, the guests peered curiously at the interior. Some nodded with approval at the brocaded settees and potted plants in the ground-floor lobby. Others went upstairs, where they examined the rows of tidy beds and washstands lining the bright, curtained wards on the second and third floors.

Dr. Elizabeth Blackwell observed the crowd and enjoyed the admiring comments of her many friends and guests. She had worked long and hard for this event—the opening of the New York Infirmary for Women and Children.

As Blackwell greeted her guests, she looked back on the efforts that had preceded this moment. Eight years earlier, in 1849, she had become the first woman to graduate from a medical school in America. In the period that followed, she faced many obstacles as she struggled to get the practical training that she needed to become a doctor.

Her pioneering steps had destroyed some of the barriers that kept women out of the medical profession. Now Blackwell hoped that *this* pioneering step— the opening of a hospital that would be administered by women doctors for women patients—would break down still more barriers.

Blackwell wanted her hospital to lead the way in allowing female medical school graduates to receive practical medical training equal to the kind of training that male graduates received. She also hoped to use the new hospital facilities to improve health care for women, particularly poor women. And she planned to make the hospital a place where women would be educated to take more responsibility for their health and the health of their families.

Chatting with her guests, Blackwell revealed an additional goal. One day, she confided, the four small cubicles on the hospital's top floor would house medical students—*women* medical students. Blackwell was planning to open a new medical school exclusively for the education of women.

Blackwell's guests understood the importance of what she had already accomplished—and what she still sought to achieve. In nineteenth-century America, women were respected as care-givers and nurturers, but they were treated as second-class citizens. They could not vote or hold public office. According to the law, an unmarried woman was the responsibility of her closest male relative; most married women had no control over their own property—and little control over their own lives.

In 1845, when Elizabeth Blackwell first began to dream of becoming a doctor, women had few chances to get an education beyond elementary school. At that time, many people didn't believe that women could stand the strain of studying difficult subjects, such as chemistry or mathematics, to say nothing of anatomy and other subjects essential to the study of medicine.

To marry and have children was assumed to be the goal of every young girl. A woman's education was meant to prepare her for marriage, not for what was considered to be a "masculine" career. Those few women who pursued such careers confronted difficult challenges. Since they were not admitted to most high schools and colleges, they could not receive the training needed to become doctors, lawyers, ministers, or members of other "masculine" professions.

As she spoke with her guests, Elizabeth Blackwell reminded them of the advice she had received when trying to convince medical schools to admit her. "You should become a nurse," she was told. Or, "Attend a school overseas." "Disguise yourself as a man," others had suggested.

Elizabeth Blackwell had applied to many colleges before she found a medical school that would allow her to enroll. Even then, she was finally admitted only because the students of Geneva College thought that the idea of a female medical student was a good joke. But Blackwell graduated at the head of her class in 1849. The students who had laughed heartily at the idea that she might graduate beside them were proud to stand with her.

Blackwell opened the doors of America's medical schools to other women students. Her younger sister Emily followed her into medicine and became one of the first female surgeons in America. By 1899, 50 years after Blackwell received her medical degree, women made up 10 percent of the students in the country's medical schools. In some large cities, as many as 18 percent of all physicians were women. These numbers show that women had won the opportunity to receive medical education. They had changed people's minds about what women could do.

When Elizabeth Blackwell began her work, few in the medical world or among the public welcomed the idea of a woman doctor. She encountered great resistance—and much of it came from women. Blackwell remembered her visit to the famous English actress Fanny Kemble to ask for funds for the new infirmary. Kemble listened "with kindness," Blackwell recalled. But when Kemble heard "that the physicians of the hospital were to be women, she sprang up to her full height, turned her flashing eyes upon us, and with the deepest tragic tones of her magnificent voice, she exclaimed: 'Trust a woman—as a doctor!—NEVER!' "

But on that sunny day in 1857, when the doors of her infirmary opened, Blackwell felt that her struggle to change the popular opinion so forcefully expressed by Fanny Kemble was nearing an end. As she led her friends to the fourth floor to view the space set aside for future students, Elizabeth Blackwell was confident she was winning the battle that she had fought for so many years.

The crowd moved outside the building to hear several distinguished speakers dedicate the hospital. Rev. Henry Ward Beecher spoke eloquently, his deep voice rising with passion. "Woman has a right to do whatever she can do well," Rev. Beecher proclaimed to an appreciative audience. "I welcome everything that tends to enlarge the sphere of her development. I am sure this infirmary will grow and prosper."

Finally, Elizabeth Blackwell herself addressed the crowd. At 36, Blackwell was proud of her efforts, she told her audience, but she knew that the path ahead for women would not be an easy or smooth one. "The full, thorough education of women in medicine is a new idea," Blackwell remarked, "and, like all other truths, requires time to prove its value."

But she looked forward to the challenges yet to come. Her blue-gray eyes shining, Elizabeth Blackwell was ready to face the future, ready to help time prove the value of her cause.

2

"Little Shy"

The year was 1832. More than 200 passengers crowded aboard the ship *Cosmo* among the piles of luggage and the crates of salt beef, crackers, pork, and other supplies. A cow had been brought on board to provide milk for the passengers. The August breeze caught the ship's canvas sails, and the rigging creaked and groaned. Friends and relatives waved good-bye as the merchant ship pulled away from the dock.

Eleven-year-old Elizabeth Blackwell watched the familiar harbor of her English home disappear on the horizon. Along with seven brothers and sisters, her mother and father, four aunts, and a governess, she was setting out for New York.

Born on February 3, 1821, near the city of Bristol, England, Elizabeth was the third child of Hannah and Samuel Blackwell. She had two older sisters, Marian and Anna, and five younger siblings—Samuel, Henry, Emily, Ellen, and John Howard. (Three other children had died in infancy.) Years later, Elizabeth described her family as bound by "strong ties of natural affection" and "surrounded by wholesome influences."

One of these wholesome influences, according to Elizabeth, was religion. Every Sunday, Samuel and his family went to Bristol's Bridge Street Chapel for both morning and afternoon services. Samuel himself led the prayers at times. At home, the children were required to attend daily prayer meetings before breakfast. At night, Hannah gathered the children around her and read to them from a book of moral tales.

Unlike most English families, the Blackwells did not follow the practices of the Church of England, the officially recognized church. Instead, they belonged to a religious group called the Dissenters. The Dissenters received their name because they dissented from, or opposed, the established church.

Because many schools did not admit Dissenters, the Blackwells hired tutors to educate their children at home. It was not unusual for parents in the 1800s to have their children privately tutored, but it was very uncommon to educate girls in the same way as boys. Generally, in nineteenth-century England, only young boys received a well-rounded education. Girls were taught those skills viewed as necessary to make them good wives and mothers.

But the Blackwells were a most unusual family. Samuel and Hannah believed that men and women should be treated as equals; they insisted that their sons and daughters be taught the same subjects at the same pace. So, together, the Blackwell girls and boys studied history, astronomy, mathematics, foreign languages, and other subjects.

As Elizabeth later wrote, the Blackwell children enjoyed "a passion for reading." Their own "pocket money," she recalled, "was spent in buying books." A new book was considered to be "the greatest delight." Elizabeth never lost this love of the written word. In later years, she read everything she could, from the essays of the American writer Ralph Waldo Emerson to President Andrew Jackson's memoirs. She devoted time to her own writing as well, from pamphlets on medical issues to her autobiography.

The principle of equality was a guiding rule in the Blackwell home. Unlike most English parents in the 1800s, Samuel and Hannah allowed the children to join them at dinner, even when guests were visiting. The children especially looked forward to these evening gatherings. "To be allowed to dine and listen at a side-table," Elizabeth said, "was indeed a treat."

Elizabeth never forgot the evening when she was banished from the dining room by her Aunt Barbara. Aunt Bar, who lived with the family, was the "stern though upright ruler" of the older Blackwell children, as Hannah was usually busy caring for the younger ones. Aunt Bar kept a complete record of childish misbehaviors in her dreaded "Black Book." For each misdeed, she would hand out a suitable punishment.

The evening that Aunt Bar sent Elizabeth to the attic without dinner made a profound impression on the little girl. Long after Elizabeth forgot why she had been punished, she remembered how lonely and forlorn she felt as she strained to catch a glimpse of the dinner table:

Upstairs in the dark I leaned over the banister, watched the light stream out from the dining-room as the servants carried the dishes in and out, and listened to the cheerful buzz of voices and frequent peals of laughter as the door opened. I felt very miserable, with also a sense of guilt that I should have been so wicked as to let my name get into the Black Book, for I always accepted, without thought of resistance, the decrees of my superiors.

Although she was a quiet child, Elizabeth had a streak of steady determination that could sometimes frustrate Aunt Bar. But these same qualities delighted her father. Samuel Blackwell called her "Bessie" or "Little Shy."

Elizabeth, in turn, loved and greatly admired her father. Many of her early memories were of her "dear father with his warm affection, his sense of fun, and his talent for rhyming."

One of these memories involved a telescope that Elizabeth and her older sisters, Anna and Marian, had propped up in an attic window. The window wasn't quite high enough to allow the adventurous girls a clear view of the woods beyond their house. So they sent their father a letter—a "petition for liberty," they called it—asking for permission to move the telescope to the narrow wooden walkway outside the window to get a better view.

Samuel Blackwell denied his daughters' petition. But he tried to ease their disappointment by sending his response in rhyme:

> *Anna, Bessie, and Polly,*
> *Your request is mere folly,*
> *The leads are too high*
> *For those who can't fly.*
> *If I let you go there,*
> *I suppose your next prayer*
> *Will be for a hop*
> *To the chimney top!*
> *So I charge you three misses,*
> *Not to show your phizes [faces]*
> *On parapet wall,*
> *Or chimney so tall,*
> *But to keep on the earth,*
> *The place of your birth.*

Fortunately, the girls' curiosity about the outside world could be satisfied in less dangerous ways. They often explored the "delightfully free and open" neighborhoods of Bristol. Elizabeth later recalled how these walks left them with "a charming picture-gallery" of memories. Their favorite stroll led to an estate where they admired peacocks; then, they went along a path "where violets grew on the grassy banks and natural curiosities could be collected." Such adventures gave the young Elizabeth Blackwell "endless delight" and "helped to create an early love of Nature."

While these wholesome influences produced a warm and rewarding home life, the older Blackwell children were nevertheless aware of problems in the world outside their home. "Echoes from the outside world came to us," Elizabeth said. One of these echoes involved the practice of slavery.

Bristol was an important center of sugar refining as well as an old slave-trading port. Although Britain had passed a law in 1807 outlawing the buying and selling of slaves, many of Bristol's sugar refiners chose to ignore the law and took part in the "triangular" slave trade.

As the first part of the slave trade, a ship called a slaver was loaded in a British port with goods such as cloth or weapons. The ship sailed to a port in western Africa. There, the ship's captain traded his cargo for Africans who had been enslaved. On the second leg of the journey, the slaves bought in Africa were carried to the British West Indies, where they were usually sold to work on sugar cane plantations. To conclude the triangular trade, sugar cane from the plantations was loaded into the slave ship's now empty hold and shipped to England to be refined into sugar.

Samuel Blackwell, a sugar refiner, was disturbed by the industry's role in the slave trade. He hoped one day to introduce a new process of refining sugar that would replace the cane with sugar beets. Since sugar beets could be grown in a variety of climates, Samuel hoped that beet sugar might be produced in regions where slavery was not a common practice.

As Elizabeth observed, Samuel Blackwell "early enlisted" his children in the struggle against slavery. The children, clearly understanding the moral nature of this struggle, chose to protest the slave trade and slavery by giving up sugar, which they objected to as a "slave product."

The Blackwell children were also aware that, like much of England, Bristol was undergoing hard times. For years, the economy of England had been changing in a process called the Industrial Revolution. Beginning in the early 1700s, this "revolution" transformed English society. No longer did most people earn a living as farmers or craftsmen. Now huge industries turned out products once made in the small shops of the English countryside.

Many new machines were invented as part of this process. Housed in factories, these inventions could manufacture goods faster and cheaper than the most skilled craftsman could make by hand. Soon, tens of thousands of people flocked from the country to the city to seek work in the new factories.

But there were more job seekers than jobs, and living conditions in the cities were desperately poor and crowded. Factory wages were so low that entire families, including very young children, were forced to work many hours, and often at dangerous tasks, to make enough money to survive.

These conditions created serious social tensions, which only increased when England was hurt by the economic depression of the early 1830s. In October of 1831, riots brought violence and chaos to a number of British cities, including Bristol. In the midst of the rioting, Samuel and his Dissenter friends took action.

An angry crowd had set fire to much of the town and wanted to burn down the city's ancient cathedral. Arms linked, the Dissenters stood in front of the great wooden doors of the cathedral and succeeded in stopping the mob from destroying the building.

During this incident, most of the Blackwells were staying at a rented farmhouse about nine miles from the city. Elizabeth fearfully watched black smoke pour from the heart of Bristol—and prayed for the safety of her father and his friends.

Soon after the riots ended, Samuel's sugar business underwent a devastating reversal of fortune. He lost almost all of his money. Faced with bankruptcy, Samuel Blackwell decided to move his family to the United States. He had business contacts there—fellow religious dissenters (known as Quakers). In the "land of liberty," Samuel assured his family, the Blackwells would start over.

So, on that August morning in 1832, the Blackwell family boarded the *Cosmo*. Years later, Elizabeth remembered the "delightful experiences" the younger children had during the crossing. But Anna, the oldest child, was seasick much of the time. She recalled a very different journey. She described her disgust with the "horrid, stinking, filthy" cabins and the slapping of the canvas sails that sounded "like curses."

Aside from a few bouts of seasickness, the Blackwells survived the seven-week voyage in good health. On a bright October day, they spotted the outline of New York's longed-for shore on the horizon. Samuel watched as his family studied the approaching city. Although they uttered scarcely a word, Samuel could easily read their emotions. "The fixed and eager eye, and the gushing tear," he recalled, "told their feelings better than words."

3

A Greater Purpose

Life was hectic for the Blackwells in the bustle of New York City. Soon after their arrival, Hannah and Samuel's ninth child, George Washington Blackwell, was born. (He was called "Washy" by his family.) As the family settled into their busy and crowded house, Samuel began to rebuild his business with help from his Quaker contacts.

The Blackwells found more space for themselves when they moved, in 1834, to New Jersey. Here, the children could spend the long summer hours hiking through nearby fields and forests. During the winter, they delighted in sleighing and ice skating. Taking the ferry to New York City was always an adventure.

The new life that America offered the Blackwells, however, resembled the "Old World" in some unhappy ways. Again, the Blackwells had to confront the problem of slavery. Slavery was widespread in the southern states, where white plantation owners relied on African slave labor to produce rice, tobacco, sugar cane, and cotton. Opposition to slavery had begun as early as the 1600s. By the end of the eighteenth century, the opponents of slavery (known as abolitionists because they wanted to abolish, or end, the practice) had succeeded in passing laws that outlawed slavery in several of the states. But in the 1830s, slavery was still legal in most of the country.

The Blackwells joined the growing opposition to the practice of keeping slaves. Their home was always open to abolitionists. Among the anti-slavery leaders who regularly visited the family was William Lloyd Garrison, a noted editor who vigorously condemned slavery in his newspaper, *The Liberator*. Elizabeth was soon involved in the cause—entering "ardently into the anti-slavery struggle," she wrote.

During these years, Elizabeth and her two older sisters, Anna and Marian, enjoyed a great deal of personal freedom. Years later, Elizabeth remarked that at this time "habits of unconscious independence among the sisters were formed." This habit of independence grew, and the Blackwell sisters were drawn to another reform movement gaining momentum in the United States during the 1800s—the women's movement for equal rights.

Many leaders of the women's rights movement were Quakers. Almost all had been involved in the abolitionist movement. While arguing for the equality of the races, these women had become aware of their own unequal position within American society. If the United States were truly a democracy, they argued, then women would enjoy the same rights as men, including the right to vote.

In the midst of such social debate, an economic depression swept across the country, reminding the Blackwells of the conditions that had driven them out of England. When a fire destroyed one of Samuel's sugar refineries in 1837, a frustrated and disappointed Samuel decided to move to Cincinnati, Ohio. He had heard positive accounts of freedom and opportunity there. Elizabeth recorded the details of their journey to this "small but flourishing town":

> We were delighted with the magnificent scenery of the mountains and rivers as we crossed Pennsylvania by canal and stage (for it was before the time of railways), and sailed down the noble Ohio River, then lined with forests. With eager enjoyment of new scenes, the prosperous little Western town was reached. It was picturesquely situated on a plateau, overlooking the river, and surrounded by pleasant hills.

Samuel was confident that this town would be an ideal spot for his business. Now 17, Elizabeth shared her father's sense of "hope and eager anticipation" as the Blackwells headed west, despite the fact that her sisters Anna and Marian had decided to remain in New York.

Elizabeth's optimism was short-lived. Only three months after arriving in Cincinnati in 1838, her father became sick. Samuel Blackwell died during the evening of August 7. Elizabeth sat beside him, holding his hand. He was 48 years old.

The sudden loss was a great blow to the Blackwell family. Elizabeth felt "as if all hope and joy were gone and nought was left but to die also."

"I hated the light and the beautiful day and the people who stared at us," she wrote. "I seemed alone in the world."

But the young Blackwells had little time to mourn their father's death. "Recovering from the first effects of the stunning blow," Elizabeth recalled, "we began to realize our position." Samuel had left his family "entirely unprovided for." Forced to "face the stern realities of life," the Blackwells quickly devised ways to earn money.

Elizabeth's 14-year-old brother, Samuel, took a job as a bookkeeper, and Henry, at age 13, became an errand boy for a local shop. Elizabeth and her mother opened a boarding school in their home, and Anna and Marian moved from New York to Ohio to help.

For the next several years, Elizabeth later wrote, the Blackwell women "managed to support the family and maintain a home." Finally, in 1844, with Samuel and Henry earning more money, the boarding school was closed. Elizabeth, now 23 years old, left home for western Kentucky, where she had been asked to take charge of a girls' school in the town of Henderson.

This was Elizabeth's first separation from her family. She kept up a constant correspondence from what she called the "dirty, little, straggling country village" of Henderson.

Elizabeth found the people of western Kentucky "uninteresting, with nothing to do but knit," but they were fascinated by her. "I am amused to learn how I have been talked over in every direction," she wrote, "and my teeth are particularly admired in peculiarly Kentucky style. 'Well, I do declare she's got a clean mouth, hasn't she!'—white teeth seeming remarkable where all use tobacco!"

Elizabeth Blackwell was distressed by her "first practical experience of negro slavery." In one letter, she recalled an incident that was typical of what she described as "the crude civilization of a slave state":

> I well remember sitting with my hostess who was reclining in her rocking chair, on the broad, shaded veranda, one pleasant Sunday morning, listening to the distant church bells and the rustling of the locust leaves. The eldest daughter, a tall, graceful girl, dressed for Sunday, in fresh and floating drapery, came into the veranda on

*her way to church. Just at that moment a shabby,
forlorn-looking negro in dirty rags approached
the veranda; he was one of the slaves working on
the plantation. His errand was to beg the mistress
to let him have a clean shirt on that Sunday
morning.*

*The contrast of the two figures, the young
lady and the slave, and the sharp reprimand with
which his mistress from her rocking-chair drove
the slave away, left a profound impression on my
mind. Kind as the people were to me personally,
the sense of justice was continually outraged.*

Following her first term in Henderson, Elizabeth
decided that she could no longer tolerate these daily
injustices. "To live in the midst of beings degraded to
the utmost in body and mind, utterly unable to help
them," she said, "is to me dreadful, and what I would
not do long for any consideration."

Elizabeth returned to her family and the welcome
atmosphere of Cincinnati. But she soon began to long
for a greater purpose in her life. "My brothers were
engaged in business," she wrote, "my sisters various-
ly occupied, the family life was full and active, and for
a while I keenly enjoyed the return home. But I soon
felt the want of a more engrossing pursuit."

At age 24, Elizabeth Blackwell was searching for
something "to engross my thoughts, some object in

life which will fill this vacuum and prevent this sad wearing away of the heart."

During this restless period, Elizabeth paid a visit to a family friend, Mary Donaldson, who was dying of cancer. Elizabeth was astonished when her friend turned to her and remarked: "You are fond of study, have health and leisure; why not study medicine? If I could have been treated by a lady doctor, my worst sufferings would have been spared me."

The thought of being a doctor was a startling one. "I at once repudiated the suggestion as an impossible one," Elizabeth noted, "saying I hated everything connected with the body and could not bear the sight of a medical book." However, it was an idea that simply would not fade from her thoughts. "I resolutely tried for weeks to put the idea away," Elizabeth said, "but it constantly recurred to me."

"As the idea seemed to gain force," she recalled, she "consulted with several physicians, known to my family, in various parts of the country, as to the possibility of a lady becoming a doctor." The physicians were unanimous in their response. Elizabeth was told that "there was no way of obtaining such an education for a woman; the education required was long and expensive; there were innumerable obstacles in the way of such a course." These physicians warned Elizabeth that for a woman to become a doctor was "impossible to accomplish."

As Elizabeth discovered, many people at the time believed that women lacked the intellect, the strength, and the independence of mind to perform well as doctors. Others argued that if women were allowed to develop their minds and pursue serious careers outside the home, the family structure would collapse. Some went so far as to claim that higher education and training would drain women of the energy that they needed in order to have children.

Even Elizabeth's friends were not very encouraging. One friend, for instance, warned Elizabeth of the "strong prejudice which would exist," a prejudice that Elizabeth "must either crush or be crushed by."

But Elizabeth refused to be discouraged by such arguments. She wrote that they were, in fact, "rather an encouragement than otherwise." She saw the lack of opportunity for women in the medical profession as a form of social injustice—and she was determined not to let that injustice stand. "The idea of winning a doctor's degree gradually assumed the aspect of a great moral struggle," she said, "and the moral fight possessed immense attraction for me."

To begin the struggle, Elizabeth needed to overcome two major hurdles. She needed about $3,000—a huge sum of money in those days—to pay for medical school. And before she could be admitted to medical school, she needed three years of preparatory training by a doctor. She decided to accept a teacher's position in a school in Asheville, North Carolina. There, as she noted, "whilst accumulating money for future use, I could also commence a trial of medical study, for the Reverend John Dickson, the principal of the school, had previously been a doctor."

It was a difficult change for her, but Elizabeth's decision to pursue this moral struggle gave her, then and later, a deep and lasting strength:

> *My old diary of those years vividly portrays the anxiety and painful effort with which I left the family circle and ordinary social life, and took the first step in my future medical career. I felt that I was severing the usual ties of life, and preparing to act against my strongest natural inclinations. But a force stronger than myself, then and afterwards, seemed to lead me on; a purpose was before me which I must inevitably seek to accomplish.*

Elizabeth Blackwell was once again leaving her family. "With loving good-byes and some tears," she wrote, "I left home for my unknown career."

4

Student Number 130

On June 16, 1845, accompanied by her brothers Samuel and Howard, Elizabeth Blackwell set out for an "unknown career" in North Carolina. The horse-drawn carriage pounded over rutted dirt roads, jolted across rocky creek beds, and struggled to climb the mountains of Kentucky and Tennessee. Its passengers were bounced from floor to ceiling.

But the uncomfortable journey had its rewards. "Looking down upon an ocean of mountain ridges," Blackwell wrote, "remains a wonderful panorama in memory." Samuel Blackwell recorded in his journal that Elizabeth was so moved by this scene that she climbed down from the carriage and did a dance right in the middle of the road!

After many days of traveling, the group finally reached its destination. They were welcomed at the home of Rev. Dickson. However, on the night of her brothers' departure, Elizabeth Blackwell felt a terrifying sense of dread and loneliness. For the rest of her life, this episode was as "real and vivid" to Elizabeth as when it occurred. "I was overwhelmed," she said, "with sudden terror of what I was undertaking."

In this moment of "doubt and dread," Elizabeth Blackwell turned to her usual source of consolation. "In an agony of mental despair," she said, "I cried out, 'God, help me, support me!' "

Her prayer seemed to be answered:

> *Suddenly, overwhelmingly, an answer came. A glorious presence, as of brilliant light, flooded my soul. There was nothing visible to the physical sense; but a spiritual influence so joyful, gentle, but powerful, surrounded me that the despair which had overwhelmed me vanished.*

Elizabeth Blackwell no longer feared the course she had set for herself:

> *All doubt as to the future, all hesitation as to the rightfulness of my purpose, left me, and never in afterlife returned. I knew that, however insignificant my individual effort might be, it was in a right direction.*

With a renewed sense of purpose, Blackwell went on to spend a pleasant few months with the Dicksons. The friendly household included the minister's kind wife and their young son. Rev. Dickson helped Blackwell with her medical studies, and her teaching duties went smoothly.

Asheville, like Henderson, Kentucky, was a slave society. Uncomfortable as always in the presence of slavery, Blackwell decided to make some effort on the slaves' behalf. At first, she hoped to teach the slaves to read and write, "as the only way I could reconcile it to my conscience to live amongst them." But when she learned that North Carolina law prohibited that plan, Blackwell established a Sunday school for the slaves.

Her teaching career was interrupted when Rev. Dickson, sick and overworked, decided to close his school. He urged Blackwell to go to Charleston, South Carolina, where his brother, Dr. Samuel Dickson, was known as one of the region's best doctors. In January of 1846, Blackwell set out by stagecoach, "exchanging the fine mountain country for the level rice-fields of South Carolina."

For 17 months, Elizabeth Blackwell led a pleasant and active life in Charleston. She always made time in her busy schedule to write her family. "I think of old family ties," she said in one of her letters, "and the merry old times."

But she also knew that those "merry old times" were now part of the past. "I am quite satisfied that my childhood has gone," Blackwell wrote. "I never wish to recall it, happy as it was. I want to be up and doing, not simply enjoying myself; if I never succeed in accomplishing all my intentions, I mean to have the assurance that I have done my best."

In November of 1846, Blackwell wrote home that she was more determined than ever to become a doctor. "My mind is fully made up," she wrote, "and I have not the slightest hesitation on the subject. The thorough study of medicine I am quite resolved to go through with."

A confident Elizabeth Blackwell added that she felt "fully equal to the contest."

By May 1847, she had saved enough money from her teaching to devote herself to the challenge of gaining entrance to medical school. She decided that her best opportunity lay in Philadelphia, which was, as Blackwell observed, "then considered the chief seat of medical learning in America."

In Philadelphia, Blackwell stayed at the home of a Quaker couple, Dr. William Elder and his wife. The Elders soon became Blackwell's "warm and steadfast friends," and Dr. Elder "took a generous interest" in her plans, supporting her "by encouragement through months of efforts and refusals."

As part of the admission process, Blackwell met with several of the schools' professors. The interviews were disappointing.

Some professors suggested that Blackwell go to Paris, where she might be allowed to attend medical school classes. When one doctor told her that Paris was such a "horrible place" and so completely unfit for a woman that she must abandon her plans for a medical education, Blackwell's response was clear: "I told the Doctor that if the path of duty led me to hell, I would go there."

Other doctors suggested that Blackwell disguise herself as a man to get the training she needed. But she would not make this compromise. "Neither the advice to go to Paris nor the suggestion of disguise tempted me for a moment," Blackwell insisted.

Blackwell had a point to make—at home and as a woman. "It was to my mind," she wrote, "a moral crusade on which I had entered, a course of justice and common sense. It must be pursued in the light of day, and with public sanction, in order to accomplish its end."

It was clear that Blackwell would not be accepted by any of Philadelphia's schools. She then applied for admission to the medical schools of New England— and again with unsuccessful results. At this point, Dr. Elder suggested that she look into some of the smaller medical colleges, called "country schools." Blackwell applied to 12 of these schools, bringing the total number of her applications to 29.

Finally, in late October 1847, Blackwell received a letter from the dean of Geneva College, located in northern New York state. She had been accepted into the school's medical department.

The dean wrote to Blackwell that the professors had permitted the students to resolve the matter "on their own behalf, without any interference on the part of the faculty."

Years later, Dr. Stephen Smith, a medical student at Geneva College during this time, described the circumstances surrounding Blackwell's acceptance. The faculty, Smith recalled, had assumed that the students would not allow a woman in their class. Many of the young men thought that the application was a joke.

The students drafted a document in which they accepted Blackwell as a member of their class, declaring that "to every branch of scientific education the door should be open equally to all." This document was composed in a humorous spirit, but the school's dean accepted the judgment of the medical students and sent a copy of their letter to Blackwell. It became one of her "most valued possessions."

Elizabeth Blackwell wasted no time in accepting the invitation to study at Geneva College. Traveling all night, she reached the school on November 6, 1847. After being enrolled as "Student Number 130," she moved into a nearby boarding house. "With hope and zeal and thankful feelings of rest," Blackwell wrote, "I settled down to study."

The presence of a woman medical student was the cause of much excitement and a little confusion. "I believe the professors do not exactly know in what

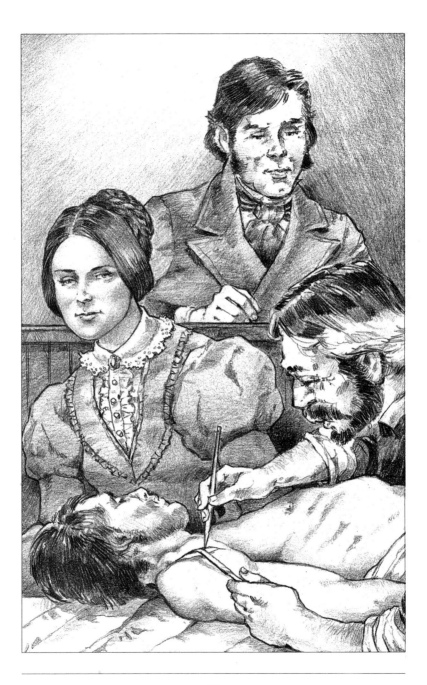

species of the human family to place me, and the students are bewildered," Blackwell wrote.

The students and professors accepted Blackwell's presence much more readily, however, than did the townspeople of Geneva, who stopped to stare at her "as at a curious animal." She did her best to shut out "the unfriendliness of the people" by "hastening daily to college as to a sure refuge."

"I knew when I shut the great doors behind me," she wrote, "that I shut out all unkindly criticism."

In her journal, Blackwell kept a record of daily frustrations and rare triumphs. On one occasion, Dr. Webster, the school's professor of anatomy, asked that Blackwell not attend some demonstrations. Blackwell recorded in her journal how she worked to change the professor's mind:

> *November 24—I told him that I was there as a student with an earnest purpose, and as a student I should be regarded; and the suggestion to absent myself from any lectures seemed to me a grave mistake. I did not wish to do so, but would yield to any wish of the class if it was their desire. I stayed in the ante-room whilst the note was being read. I listened joyfully to the very hearty approbation with which it was received by the class, and then entered the amphitheater and quietly resumed my place.*

As a female medical student, Elizabeth Blackwell felt a special commitment to her women patients. A journal entry for December 4, 1847, records how Dr. Webster sent for Blackwell "to examine the case of a poor woman." The examination was "horrible," she wrote. Blackwell thought that it was "indecent for any poor woman to be subjected to such a torture."

The words of her friend Mary Donaldson—"If I could have been treated by a lady doctor, my worst sufferings would have been spared me"— could not have been far from Blackwell's mind. "I felt more than ever the necessity of my mission," she wrote.

But that mission was a lonely one, at times an overwhelmingly lonely one. Blackwell's journal entry for December 4 continued to describe her solitude: "I went home out of spirits, I hardly know why. I felt alone. I must work by myself all life long."

Her spirits improved, however, when Elizabeth received the Blackwell family's "Christmas Annual," a holiday collection of letters, poems, and drawings. After buying herself 25 cents' worth of almonds and raisins, Elizabeth "had quite a cozy time" reading the annual on Christmas Day.

She learned that Anna was working in New York City. Henry was courting Lucy Stone, a well-known feminist. And Emily was a teacher, but she hoped one day to become a doctor like her older sister.

Blackwell was soon writing that she felt "perfectly at home" among her fellow students. As the school term came to a close in January, she felt "sad when the lectures ended" and expressed "regret at parting from friends." Since the second term would not begin until the fall, Blackwell returned to the Elders' home in Philadelphia.

There, she went to work in the hospital ward of the Blockley Almshouse, a large poorhouse built to shelter those who were too poor or too sick to find help elsewhere. Working directly with patients, Blackwell gained some of the practical, hands-on medical experience missing from her studies at college.

The Blockley Almshouse was a world unlike any that Blackwell had seen before. Patients were huddled along corridor walls, waiting for medical treatment. Stretchers lined the hallways, and the sick were left unattended. Crowds of small children—dirty, hungry, sick, and frightened—wandered here and there. The "almshouse smell" was everywhere.

Blackwell was assigned to the ward for women, most of whom were uneducated and poor. She felt powerless to help them, however. "This is horrible!" she wrote. Blackwell insisted that "women must open their eyes" to their own health concerns, that women must start to be in charge of their own health. "But how?" she wondered.

Blackwell's days at Blockley were difficult. The male students resented her presence. "When I walked into the wards," she noted, "they walked out." And while Blackwell worked at Blockley, the hospital was overwhelmed by a wave of immigrants suffering from typhus. The doctors worked day and night, but the epidemic took many lives.

At summer's end, Blackwell was glad to return to the "healthy and hopeful college life." Plans for the future increasingly occupied her time. In November, she jotted these words in her journal: "Alone all day in my room, yet anything but lonely. Bright visions of usefulness have been floating round me." Ready for the future, she was prepared to devote herself "to the accomplishment of a great idea."

One day, Blackwell witnessed an operation on a young blind girl. "Poor child! She has no protector, within or without," Blackwell wrote. "These are the women that I long to surround with my stronger arm. Alas! how almost hopeless does the task seem!"

During December and the beginning of January, Blackwell prepared for the final examinations. "I lived in my room and my college, and the outside world made little impression on me," she said. Blackwell did not find the examinations to be difficult. "Still," she wrote to her mother, "the anxiety and effort were as great as if everything were at stake."

"Hurrah, 'tis almost over!" was Blackwell's journal entry for January 22, 1849. To the delight of her fellow students, she received the top honors. She was astonished that none of the men in the class seemed envious of her. "They all seem to like me," Blackwell confided to her mother, "and I believe I shall receive my degree with their united approval."

Elizabeth Blackwell received her degree the next day, January 23, 1849. Her brother Henry, who had traveled to Geneva to attend his sister's graduation, described the ceremony in a letter home:

After a short discourse by Dr. Hale, the President, the diplomas were conferred—four being called up at a time. The President addressed them in a Latin formula, taking off his hat, but remaining seated, and so handed them their diplomas, which they received with a bow and retired. Elizabeth was left to the last and called up alone. The President, taking off his hat, rose, and addressing her in the same formula, substituting Domina for Domine, presented her the diploma, whereupon our Sis, who had walked up and stood before him with much dignity, bowed and half turned to retire, but suddenly turning back replied: "Sir, I thank you; by the help of the Most High it shall be the effort of my life to shed honor upon your diploma."

Although her completion of a medical education was a remarkable step toward equality for women, Elizabeth Blackwell described her graduation as the "first step only." She believed that "much more medical experience than I possessed was needed before the responsibilities of practice could be justly met." Blackwell had decided to be a surgeon—the first woman surgeon—and she knew that her goal would require a great deal of practical experience.

For a while after graduating, Blackwell attended medical lectures in Philadelphia. But Blackwell soon realized that she would not be able to gain practical medical training in the United States. "I felt keenly," she wrote, "the need of much wider opportunities for study than were open to women in America."

So when a cousin invited her to travel to England with him, Blackwell agreed eagerly. After a farewell visit to her family—"I could not keep down the tears," she wrote—she joined her cousin in Boston.

In April of 1849, they boarded a ship bound for England. "Beautiful Boston Bay vanished in the distance," Elizabeth wrote in her journal. "America, that land of memories, was left far behind."

5

The "Lady" Doctors

On April 30, 1849, Elizabeth Blackwell arrived in Liverpool, England. She spent her first two weeks at her cousin's country home. "I began to make acquaintance with the wonderful and unknown Old World, which I had left when a child of eleven," she recalled. "Everything seemed new and striking." She traveled on to London, and then to Paris. As she later wrote, Paris seemed to promise a world of opportunity:

> *My teachers and medical friends in America had strongly advised my going to Paris, as the one place where I should be able to find unlimited opportunities for study in any branch of medical art. Being then desirous of pursuing surgery as well as medicine, I followed their advice. I found myself in the unknown world of Paris, bent upon the one object of pursuing my studies.*

Elizabeth was soon joined in Paris by her oldest sister, Anna, who was now working as a newspaper reporter. They shared an apartment while Elizabeth looked for a hospital where she could receive practical medical training. But the French hospitals proved no more receptive to a woman studying medicine than American ones. Blackwell's requests to attend lectures or to accompany doctors on their daily rounds were repeatedly rejected.

Desperate to get hands-on medical experience, Elizabeth Blackwell enrolled in a training program for midwives at a maternity hospital. Inside the old, grey walls of La Maternité, she hoped to learn more about pregnancy and childbirth.

At La Maternité, Blackwell lived in a dormitory with other students—young women who were learning to deliver babies. Despite her medical degree, the authorities of the institution assigned Blackwell to the same entry-level course of study as the young French students, most of whom had little, if any, education. But Blackwell was determined to enter the program, she said, even if she was treated "as a young, ignorant French girl." At least, she wasn't entering disguised as a man!

The training program was difficult for her. There was no privacy, the food was awful, the work was hard, and there were many sleepless nights. But as Blackwell observed, "the experience was invaluable. It enabled me later to enter upon practice with a confidence in one important branch of medicine that no other period of study afforded."

Her stay at La Maternité was cut short by a tragic accident. Only four months into the training program, Blackwell caught a severe eye infection while treating an infected baby. On November 4, 1849, she wrote in her journal that she "felt all the afternoon a little grain of sand, as it were, in one eye. I was afraid to think what it might be."

The following day, Blackwell, her left eye swollen and closed, was herself a patient. She sent a note to her sister Anna who, "dreadfully shocked" at seeing Elizabeth's inflamed eye, "hid behind the curtain to cry." Day after day, a doctor tended the eye every two hours. But it was no use. As Blackwell remarked, "the disease had done its worst":

> I learned from the tone of my friends that my eye was despaired of. Ah! how dreadful it was to find the daylight gradually fading as my kind doctor bent over me, and removed with an exquisite delicacy of touch the films that had formed over the pupil! I could see him for a moment clearly, but the sight soon vanished, and the eye was left in darkness.

During the next three weeks, Blackwell remained optimistic that she would regain the vision in her left eye. "I still mean to be at no very distant day *the first lady surgeon in the world*," she insisted. But, gradually, she realized that the sight would not return to her eye. Six months after her left eye became infected, it was replaced with a glass eye.

Elizabeth Blackwell's dream of becoming a surgeon was gone. Her sister Anna described Elizabeth's grief and disappointment as "unspeakable."

So Blackwell returned to England, where she was granted permission to study "practical medicine" at St. Bartholomew's, one of the large London hospitals. "Every department was cordially opened to me, *except the department for female diseases!*" she complained in a letter to her family. "The Professor of Midwifery and the Diseases of Women and Children wrote me a very polite note, telling me that he entirely disapproved of a lady's studying medicine."

This was the kind of prejudice that Blackwell had encountered at every step of her career. It was never easy to accept, but Blackwell refused to let people's attitudes become an obstacle for her. "A work of ages cannot be hindered by individual feeling," she maintained. "A hundred years hence women will not be what they are."

During her stay in London, Blackwell met many of the leading figures in scientific and literary circles. She was also introduced to Florence Nightingale, who would later become famous for her own contribution to health care. The two women became good friends and spent many evenings discussing hospital reforms and the critical importance of maintaining sanitary, or clean, conditions. Blackwell later said that she owed to Florence Nightingale her own "awakening to the fact that sanitation is the supreme goal of medicine."

Practical training at St. Bartholomew's awakened Blackwell to other facts about medical care. Writing to her old friend Dr. Dickson, Blackwell admitted that she had become "very skeptical as to the wisdom of much of the practice which I see pursued every day." Hospital authorities would not listen to her ideas. A frustrated Elizabeth Blackwell came to the conclusion that her only hope for making the changes that she felt were needed in medical care would be to open her own hospital.

Elizabeth confided these plans in a letter to her sister Emily, who was studying medicine in France. Elizabeth hoped that Emily, whom she addressed as her "future partner," would help her. "I look forward with great interest to the time when you can aid me, for I have really no medical friend."

In her letter to Emily, Elizabeth expressed hope for a day "when men and women will be valuable friends in medicine." But that day, she said, would come only when more women had established themselves as competent doctors and gained professional equality. "For a time," she wrote, "that cannot be."

Blackwell thought about establishing her hospital in England. But she decided it was wiser to return to America, where women had made greater progress in medicine. She wrote that "the parting from English friends and opportunities was a painful one." But in July 1851, Elizabeth Blackwell once again sailed from England to America—and to a new start.

Blackwell described her first seven years of practice in New York as a "very difficult" period. "I had no medical companionship," she wrote. "The profession stood aloof, and society was distrustful." New York, like the rest of the nation, was simply not ready for a female physician.

Blackwell had trouble renting office space. When her practice finally opened, no one responded to the announcement that Dr. Elizabeth Blackwell was now seeing patients. And her landlady, out of spite, never delivered messages to her. "A blank wall of social and professional antagonism faces the woman physician," Elizabeth wrote to Emily.

With little medical work to do and few friends to visit, Blackwell turned her attention to the preparation of a course of lectures on the health care of young women. Young women of the time, Blackwell knew, wore tight corsets that restricted breathing, digestion, and movement. They never seemed to exercise, and because of this, they usually appeared pale and lacked energy. Most women knew very little about their own bodies and even less about women's health concerns in general.

Blackwell decided to educate women about the female body and how to care for it. In the spring of 1852, while struggling to establish her own medical practice, Blackwell delivered a series of lectures "on the physical education of girls." She spoke about the importance of sanitary grooming habits and about the need for regular exercise, a balanced diet, and properly fitted clothing. Blackwell also explained how the female reproductive system works.

Much of what Blackwell taught was considered new and daring in the 1850s. The lectures sparked so much public interest that a New York publisher later printed them under the title, *The Laws of Life in Reference to the Physical Education of Girls.* "These lectures," Blackwell noted, "owing to the social and professional connections which resulted from them, gave me my first start in practical medical life."

Many of the women who paid two dollars to hear Blackwell speak were Quakers. They soon became Dr. Elizabeth Blackwell's first patients. As Blackwell said, "My practice during those early years was very much a Quaker practice."

But she still was not earning enough money to cover her expenses. Unable to find work in a hospital, Blackwell decided to borrow the money to open her own clinic. With the support of her Quaker friends,

Elizabeth Blackwell founded the New York Dispensary for Indigent Women and Children in March 1853.

Located near Tompkins Square, in the middle of New York's immigrant slums, the clinic answered a pressing need for medical services for the poor, especially for women and children who could not afford regular health care. The dispensary's stated purpose was "to give poor women an opportunity of consulting physicians of their own sex."

Most of the patients were poor German women, many of whom had never before seen a doctor. For some, no doctors had been available. Others had been too scared or embarrassed to seek medical help from a male doctor. Slowly, these women began to come to the dispensary. By the end of its first year, the clinic had treated 200 patients.

But Blackwell did more than treat sickness. She taught her new patients about the importance of good health practices, such as cleanliness and bathing, in the prevention of diseases. She taught them how to keep a sanitary household and stressed the value of fresh air and exercise in raising healthy children.

Day and night, Elizabeth Blackwell took her message to the crowded tenements. She ventured into the neighborhoods that surrounded her clinic to assist at births, to deliver needed medical supplies, or simply to give advice.

Despite the growing success of the clinic, Blackwell often felt lonely. It seemed to be the price she had to pay for her pioneering work. "I understand now why this life has never been lived before," she wrote in a letter to Anna.

In the summer of 1853, Elizabeth was cheered by the arrival of Emily, who worked in the clinic as her assistant. But her sister soon had to return to Western Reserve Medical College in Cleveland, Ohio, to continue her studies. After Emily graduated in 1854, she followed Elizabeth's path abroad for further training.

While in Europe, Emily received a letter from an excited sister. "I have found a student in whom I can take a great deal of interest," Elizabeth wrote.

The student was a young German woman named Marie Zakrzewska. She had shown up on Elizabeth's doorstep, seeking work. Marie had been chief of midwifery at a Berlin hospital. Forced to leave when the hospital authorities objected to a woman holding such an important position, she had come to New York, hoping to find greater opportunities for women doctors. "There is true stuff in her," Elizabeth wrote, "and I shall do my best to bring it out."

Marie, in turn, could not believe her good luck. After her first meeting with Blackwell, Marie wrote in her diary, "I cannot comprehend how Dr. Blackwell could ever have taken so deep an interest in me. Yet she did." Blackwell soon helped her new friend gain entry to Western Reserve Medical College, the same school from which Emily had recently graduated.

The two women made plans to practice medicine together in the future. But that was the future. And Marie's departure for Ohio left Elizabeth alone—once again. "The utter loneliness of life," she wrote of this time, "became intolerable."

Elizabeth Blackwell had decided that she would probably never marry. Yet she wanted very much to share her life with someone. In October of 1854, she visited an orphanage for immigrant children. There, Blackwell adopted a seven-year-old named Katherine Barry. To Elizabeth, the adopted child would always be "Kitty." And to Kitty, her adoptive mother would always be "Doctor."

Kitty added joy and laughter to Elizabeth's life. "On one day," Elizabeth recalled, "she was present during the visit of a friendly physician. After he was gone, she came to me with a very puzzled face, exclaiming, 'Doctor, how very odd it is to hear a man called Doctor!' "

Two years after she had adopted Kitty, Elizabeth noted in her journal that she felt "full of hope and strength for the future."

"Who would ever guess the restorative support which that poor little orphan has been to me?" she wrote. "I desperately needed the change of thought she compelled me to give her. It was a dark time, and she did me good. Her genial and loyal temperament suited me. Now I look forward with much hope to the coming events of this year."

In 1856, a host of Blackwells came to New York to visit Elizabeth. Samuel brought with him his wife, the Rev. Antoinette Brown. Brown was the first American woman to be ordained as a minister. They were soon followed by Elizabeth's mother and sisters Ellen and Marian. Elizabeth's brother Henry and his wife, Lucy Stone, also arrived in the city. Stone was leading a crusade to gain equal rights for women.

Elizabeth was overjoyed to be surrounded by her large, close family. "I have been more than eight years without a family circle," she wrote to Emily. "I can now appreciate one as I never did before."

Emily, too, soon joined the family circle—and her sister's work. "In 1856," Elizabeth recalled, "my working powers were more than doubled by the arrival of my sister, Dr. Emily Blackwell, who became henceforth my partner and able co-worker." Shortly thereafter, Marie Zakrzewska (or "Zak," as she was called) would triple Elizabeth's "working powers" when she joined the two Blackwell sisters after her graduation from medical school.

The three women set to work on their common dream—the establishment of a new hospital run by women and for women. This hospital would be the first medical facility of its kind. "The attempt to establish a hospital conducted entirely by women excited much opposition," Elizabeth said. "Although college instruction was being given to women students, no hospital was anywhere available for practical instruction or the exercise of the woman-physician's skill."

A host of objections were raised to this new medical effort. The three partners were told that no one would rent them space for such an undertaking, that female doctors would be looked upon with so much suspicion that the police would interfere, that death certificates signed by women physicians would not be recognized, that women doctors would not be able to control their patients, and that they would never be able to raise enough money for so unpopular a goal.

They were told all these things, but they didn't listen. They persisted in their work.

Finally, in 1857, the doctors opened the doors of the New York Infirmary for Women and Children. Elizabeth chose the birthday of Florence Nightingale, May 12, as the day of the opening, in tribute to her good friend and medical colleague.

Although the hospital's board of consulting doctors included men who were highly regarded in the medical profession, the New York Infirmary was run entirely by women. Elizabeth was the hospital's director, Emily was chief surgeon, and Marie was resident physician and manager. Four female medical students served as interns and nurses.

Patients were asked to pay four dollars a week if they had the money. For those who could not pay, the care was free. Less than a month after it opened, the New York Infirmary was filled to capacity. During its first seven months, the doctors treated more than 900 patients. In the following year, 1858, more than 3,000 cases were handled. In later years, this success would mean larger quarters and additional staff.

The hospital also introduced several new medical practices considered routine today. Follow-up treatment was provided for patients after they returned to their homes, and educational programs were offered in hygiene and in disease prevention.

Among the early staff members of the hospital was Rebecca Cole, the first African-American woman doctor. Dr. Cole held the job of "sanitary visitor." In this position, modeled on the work that Elizabeth had done at the Tompkins Street clinic, Cole visited poor women in their homes and taught them ways to care for their families' health. The duties of the sanitary visitor, as Elizabeth Blackwell described them, were to give "practical instruction to mothers on the management of infants and the preservation of the health of their families."

In these years, the idea that women could become successful doctors was gaining wider acceptance. The women's medical movement was growing not only in New York, but also in Philadelphia, Boston, and other cities. But the struggle for professional equality was far from over. Several frightening incidents, in fact, threatened to put an early end to Blackwell's work at the New York Infirmary.

Marie Zakrzewska recorded one such frightening episode. After a woman died in childbirth, an angry mob gathered outside the clinic. "An immense crowd collected," Zak wrote, "hooting and yelling and trying to push in the doors."

The mob, wielding pickaxes, was convinced that the doctors were killing their patients. Amid shouts of "You killed her!" the crowd surrounded the hospital.

As the doctors tried to calm frightened patients, a tall, shovel-bearing Irishman whose family had been treated at the infirmary, pushed his way to the steps of the hospital and addressed the crowd. The "lady doctors" were good women, he said. Patients sometimes died in men's hospitals, too. This man's speech and shovel—plus the timely appearance of the city's watchman—persuaded the mob to retreat.

The greatest threat that confronted women doctors, however, was not violence. It was a pattern of discrimination that denied women equal opportunity. At the New York Infirmary's opening ceremony, Rev. Henry Ward Beecher suggested that the real sickness to be cured there was the evil of prejudice.

As a result of her own professional experiences, Elizabeth Blackwell knew only too well that women doctors would constantly have to prove their worth before they would be accepted as equal to their male colleagues. At the infirmary's opening ceremony, she spoke about the challenge ahead:

Women must show to medical men, even more than to the public, their capacity to act as physicians, their earnestness as students of medicine, before the existing institutions, with their great advantages of practice and complete organization, will be opened to them. They must prove their ability before expecting professional recognition.

The time when men and women would be equal partners in medical careers had not yet arrived. And Elizabeth Blackwell's work was not yet finished.

6

A Solid Foundation

Once the hospital was a clear success, Elizabeth and Emily began to develop the plans for their next goal—a medical college for women. They would have to work on this project without the help of Zak, who had recently accepted a position at a Boston hospital.

By 1859, 10 years after Blackwell graduated from Geneva College, hundreds of other women had been awarded medical degrees. However, most women did not receive fair treatment from coeducational schools, even when they were admitted. Two medical colleges for women had recently been started, but they were plagued by poor programs and low standards. Blackwell vowed that she would create a medical college to "give women the very highest education that modern science will afford."

She scarcely had time to lay the groundwork for the medical school before the nation exploded in 1861. The slavery issue, which had gradually divided the nation, now ignited a violent conflict—a civil war that was to last four long years. "The great catastrophe," Blackwell observed, "overwhelmed the country and dominated every other interest."

To Blackwell, the war was another moral crusade. "The war was essentially a rebellion by a portion of the States for the maintenance of slavery," she wrote. "To us, nourished from our childhood on the idea of human freedom and justice, the contest was of absorbing interest." The Blackwell sisters threw themselves "energetically into the cause of freedom."

Early in the war, Elizabeth saw that there would be an urgent demand for nurses to tend the wounded. She called an emergency meeting at the infirmary to discuss how best to meet this pressing need. To her surprise, a huge crowd of women gathered. Day after day, Blackwell interviewed the volunteers. Those who were qualified received medical training, either at the infirmary or at other New York hospitals. In addition to recruiting nurses, Elizabeth Blackwell maintained her busy schedule at the infirmary during the war. Often, she worked without rest for days on end.

When the bloodshed finally stopped in April of 1865, Elizabeth and Emily renewed their efforts to obtain support—and money—for their medical college. In 1868, their dream became a reality. That November, almost 20 years after Elizabeth had received her own medical degree at Geneva College, she presided over the opening of the Women's Medical College of the New York Infirmary.

"It has required fifteen years of patient work—work by faith (for the way has been very dark) to lay the foundation of a college," Blackwell said. "Little by little, however, we have laid one stone upon another, until we have a foundation sufficient to stand on. It is small, certainly, but solid." This new medical school, Blackwell explained, would not try simply to imitate other schools. Rather, it would improve on them.

The Women's Medical College of the New York Infirmary became the first medical school to have a professor of hygiene on its faculty. Besides teaching students how to practice cleanliness and sanitation as a form of preventive medicine, this professor would oversee the work of the sanitary visitor. "It has always seemed to me that the first aim of the family physician should be to diffuse the sanitary knowledge which would enable parents to bring up healthy children," Blackwell wrote. She herself served as the professor of hygiene during the early years of the school.

The new college was innovative in other ways as well. Unlike most medical schools, it set up rigorous entrance requirements. To gain admission, a student had to pass a tough examination. The college also extended its program to three—and later, four—years of study, instead of graduating students in the standard 10 months. The inclusion of practical experience in the

course of study was also unusual. The establishment of an examining board of doctors, separate from the school's faculty, was another important innovation. It insured that physicians who had no direct connection to the college, and therefore no stake in the outcome, determined whether or not a student was qualified to receive a medical degree.

A reporter visiting the college published a first-hand account of the school. He described a class of women standing diligently over the dissecting tables, their hair swept back in gray kerchiefs and their long, hooped skirts covered with wide aprons. On the walls behind them hung anatomy charts and a drawing of a skeleton. This, the reporter explained, was the room where the anatomy class practiced operations on dead human bodies, cutting them open in order to understand how the various parts work together.

The reporter concluded that the medical education provided at the Women's Medical College of the New York Infirmary was "equal to that of any school in the country."

7

Pioneer Work

In 1869, when Elizabeth Blackwell was 48 years old, she declared that her "pioneer work in America" had come to an end. Women's medical colleges had been established in Philadelphia, New York, and Boston. Nearly a dozen schools that had once enrolled only men were now accepting female students.

While women in the United States were making great strides in the medical field, women in England were progressing much more slowly. Confident that Emily could manage the hospital and medical college without her, Elizabeth decided to return to England. There, she hoped that she could "assist in the pioneer work so bravely commencing."

In England, Blackwell missed her family. Feeling nostalgic, one day she revisited her childhood home. Forty years had passed since "Little Shy" had played here, and Elizabeth observed that "all was changed."

But strong memories remained:

The pleasant walled-in garden across the street, with its fine fruit trees, where we played for hours together with a neighbor's children, was turned into a carpenter's yard. The long garden behind the house, with its fine trees, and stable opening into a back street, was built over; but as I stood in the hall and looked up, I suddenly seemed to see a little childish face peeping wistfully over the banister, and the whole scene of that dining-room paradise, from which the child was banished, rose vividly before me.

Soon after, Elizabeth received the sad news that her mother, Hannah, had died of a severe infection at the age of 77. Three years earlier, Elizabeth's brother Howard had also died. Over the years, she would see her family circle grow even smaller as other relatives passed away.

During these years, Elizabeth Blackwell remained in the land of her birth, where she kept herself happily active. She set up her own medical practice in London and helped found the London School of Medicine for Women, where she taught gynecology, the study of women's health.

Blackwell worked to redefine the scope of health care, making the medical community more responsive to women, children, minority groups, and the poor.

"My long-cherished conviction of the importance of the medical profession as a conservator of health constantly deepened," she wrote.

Blackwell gave lectures on "rules of health for the guidance of poor women in the management of their households." Of special concern to Blackwell was the care and health of children. "It has become clear to me," she wrote, "that our medical profession has not yet fully realized the special responsibility which rests upon it to watch over the cradle of the race." It should be part of medicine's mission, Blackwell insisted, "to see that human beings are well born, well nourished, and well educated."

Blackwell also continued her interest in the "wide diffusion of sanitary knowledge among the people." To further that end, she helped to found the National Health Society in 1871. Its motto was "Prevention is better than cure."

In her lectures and writing, she discussed family planning and sex education. Although Blackwell felt that these subjects were "the duty of the physician to discuss," not everyone shared her belief.

A pamphlet she wrote in 1876, entitled "Counsel to Parents on the Moral Education of their Children," was rejected by most publishers as too controversial. "So little at that time was the importance of sexual education understood," Blackwell wrote, "that when I read my pamphlet to a friend, she assured me that if

I published that manuscript, my name would be a forbidden word."

Blackwell's activities slowed when, in her fifties, she began suffering from health problems. Eventually, she traded the smoke and fog of the city for the fresh air and rolling countryside of southern England. She bought a home, Rock House, which was perched on a steep cliff overlooking the English Channel. From the terrace of her home, she could watch the fishermen come and go. Here, she could observe the changing moods of the sea.

Blackwell spent most of the last three decades of her life at Rock House. Kitty lived with her, and Anna and Marian settled nearby. At Rock House, Elizabeth regained enough strength to continue lecturing and writing for many years, but she gave up her private medical practice in 1894.

Meanwhile, Kitty persuaded her adoptive mother to write her life story. Published In 1895, Blackwell's autobiography was titled *Pioneer Work in Opening the Medical Profession to Women*. Elizabeth dedicated the work to Kitty. She wrote that Kitty "has proved a real daughter to me."

After Marian and Anna died, Kitty and Elizabeth began spending their summers at Kilmun, a village on the west coast of Scotland. Behind the village, Blackwell wrote, lay the inlet of Holy Loch. In the distance loomed a range of "delectable mountains."

In 1906, Elizabeth and Kitty decided to journey to the United States. Elizabeth, now 85 years old, longed to see her surviving relatives one last time. Elizabeth and Kitty stayed in the United States long enough to celebrate Emily's eightieth birthday. Then, amid tearful good-byes, Elizabeth Blackwell embarked on her last journey across the rough waters of the Atlantic.

While vacationing at Kilmun the following summer, Blackwell fell headlong down a flight of stairs. The fall so affected her that she was not able to work again. Elizabeth Blackwell spent the rest of her days watching the ocean from the Rock House terrace, only occasionally venturing out for a walk on Kitty's arm.

On May 31, 1910, Elizabeth Blackwell died of a stroke. She was 89 years old.

She was buried in the churchyard at the village of Kilmun, under the shadows of the Scottish mountains. On her headstone was inscribed:

In loving memory of Elizabeth Blackwell, M.D. Born at Bristol 3rd February, 1821, died at Hastings 31st May, 1910. The first woman of modern times to graduate in medicine (1849) and the first to be placed on the British Medical Register (1859).

8

The Last Frontiers

The day after Elizabeth Blackwell died, the *London Times* printed her obituary. It said that she had been "in the fullest sense of the word a pioneer."

Blackwell's pioneering work had transformed the public's attitude toward women entering the medical profession. She had enlarged the profession's sense of its social responsibility, insisting that decent medical care was everyone's right. She had brought attention to the vital roles that sanitation and prevention should play in medicine.

Elizabeth Blackwell herself lived to witness much of the progress that women made in the medical field. When she said, in 1849, "It shall be the effort of my life to shed honor upon your diploma," there were no certified women physicians in the United States. By 1900, there were almost 7,000. Medical associations were admitting women as members; women doctors were publishing articles in professional journals; and hospitals and medical schools were accepting women as physicians and teachers.

With the last barriers to equal education broken, the trustees of the Women's Medical College of the New York Infirmary closed the school. "The friends who established, and have supported, the Infirmary and its College," Emily Blackwell said, "have always regarded coeducation as the final stage in the medical education of women." Because women could obtain medical education in the same classes, under the same faculty, and with the same opportunities for practical training as men, there was no longer any need for a separate women's school.

The directors of other women's medical colleges shared this point of view. Of the 19 women's medical schools that were established in the 1800s, only three continued to operate into the twentieth century.

The gains that women had made in the medical profession were often challenged in the years following Elizabeth Blackwell's death. For a time, the number of female doctors in the United States declined. But the progress for which Blackwell had fought was only temporarily reversed.

Whatever the difficulties of the struggle, women would not turn back from the world of professional opportunity that had been opened to them. Today, more than 30 percent of medical students are women.

In the United States alone, more than 85,000 women are medical doctors.

At the end of her autobiography, Elizabeth Blackwell wrote that the study of medicine by women as well as men would begin a new era. She looked ahead "with hope" to the future influence of women doctors. If Elizabeth Blackwell were alive today, she would no doubt look back—at her work and the work of countless other women—with pride.

For Further Reading

The life of Elizabeth Blackwell has been covered in several full-length biographies. *A Doctor Alone*, by Peggy Chambers (Abelard-Schuman, 1958), and *Child of Destiny*, by Ishbel Ross (Harper, 1949), each provide a complete account. Blackwell is also covered in *They Dared to Be Doctors*, by Mary St. J. Fancourt (Longmans Green, 1965), and *Those Extraordinary Blackwells*, by Elinor Rice Hays (Harcourt, Brace, 1967).

Patricia Clapp has written a fictional biography in Elizabeth Blackwell's voice: *Dr. Elizabeth* (Lothrop, Lee & Shepard, 1974).

Blackwell wrote her own life story in a series of "autobiographical sketches": *Pioneer Work in Opening the Medical Profession to Women* (Schocken, 1977).

A chapter on Blackwell is included in *Great Women of Medicine*, by Ruth Fox Hume (Random House, 1964). Other chapters cover the lives of Florence Nightingale, Elizabeth Garrett Anderson, Sophia Jex Blake, Mary Putnam Jacobi, Marie Curie, and women doctors of the twentieth century.

The history of women in medicine is given more detailed treatment in several adult histories, including *Send Us a Lady Physician: Women Doctors in America, 1835-1920*, edited by Ruth J. Abram (Norton, 1985). A bibliography of "Women Heroes of Science" can be found in *Science Books & Films*, March 1991. It includes a section for young readers.

Index